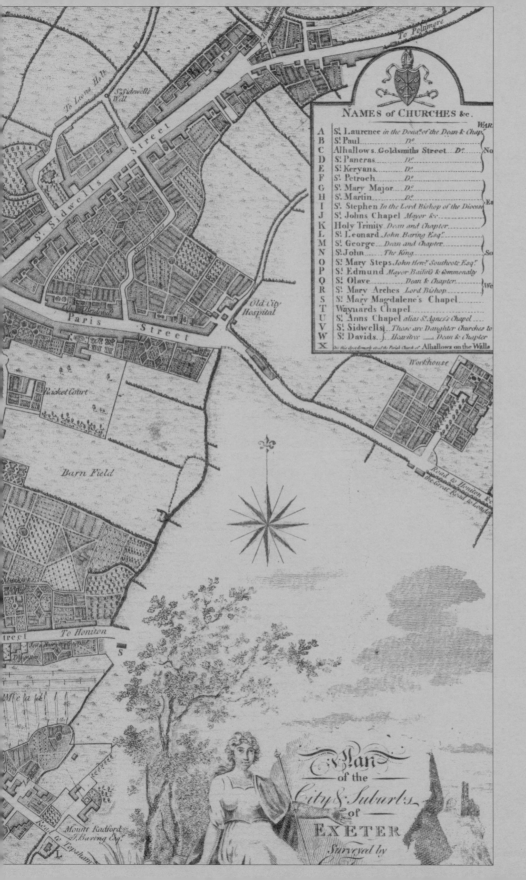

*Exeter, 1792*

# EXETER ENGRAVED

*The Secular City*

To:

John,

Just another book on Exeter!
From Killerton.

October 20th 2001.

With all my LOVE
Wendy.

# EXETER ENGRAVED

## The Secular City

Volume One

Todd Gray

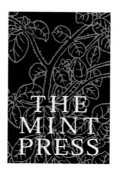

THE MINT PRESS

*For Christopher and Yon*

First published in Great Britain by The Mint Press, 2000

© Todd Gray 2000

**ISBN 1-903356-04-0**

Cataloguing in Publication Data
CIP record for this title is available from the British Library

**The Mint Press**
18 The Mint
Exeter, Devon
England EX4 3BL

Typeset in Palatino by Quince Typesetting

Jacket design by Delphine Jones

Main cover illustration, View of Northernhay, *c.*1845,
courtesy of Westcountry Studies Library

Printed and bound in Great Britain
by Short Run Press Ltd, Exeter

# Contents

# Acknowledgements

I would like to thank John Allan, Richard Ball, Stuart Blaylock, Helen James, Andy Jones, Ian Maxted, Charles Page, Tony Rouse, Margery Rowe and Caroline Worthington for their help with this book. Permission to publish illustrations has been given by the Westcountry Studies Library, the Devon & Exeter Institution and the Royal Albert Memorial Museum. Finally, I would also like to thank Exeter City Council for financial support.

# Foreword

There is a proliferation of publications which present historic photographs to the public. These images give an immediacy to the past and capture a wide range of often intimate aspects of life in bygone times. As photography is still with us, comparisons between past and present can easily be made. Photographs take the visual record of our region back to the mid-nineteenth century, although photographs before the 1880s are relatively rare. But the rise of photography coincided with the decline of a range of earlier techniques for reproducing images which carry the visual record back well into the eighteenth century and occasionally earlier: the topographical print.

This book performs a valuable service in bringing a comprehensive collection of these neglected images of Exeter together for the first time. Prints were normally a less spontaneous product than even the earliest photographs and were often a collaboration between two or more individuals, the artist who created the original drawing or painting, the engraver or lithographer who copied it laboriously in reverse onto the metal plate or lithographic stone and the publisher, who financed the printing and organized the sale. There were exceptions; etching was a medium which attracted the amateur artist and lithographers could transfer their own drawings onto stone for printing, but the considerable investment involved in producing a print meant that there was a limitation on the range of subjects that it was viable to produce. To appreciate the evolution of the subject matter over time helps us to gain an insight into the changing aesthetic perceptions of the English landscape and urban environment by the wealthier classes, who could afford to purchase the engravings. That we can trace this development for Devon is thanks in no small part to the work of John V. Somers Cocks who described 3,500 of these images in his catalogue *Devon topographical prints, 1660–1870:*

*a catalogue and guide* published in 1977 by Devon Library Services, a work which still has few parallels in other parts of the country. Through the wealth of illustrations in the present work, the development from the earliest depictions of castles and other antiquities, through the growing interest in landscape and picturesque views, to the wider range of subject matter in the series of steel engraved vignettes produced for the growing tourist market can be more easily appreciated than in the bare lists of titles of prints, valuable though these are. The images make it possible to compare the painstaking striving for accuracy of the topographical draughtsman with the subjective approach of many artists, to see how the plates could be altered to reflect these changes over time, to discover how one engraver may have copies from another. The reader can also observe the changing styles, influenced not only by changes in taste but also by the possibilities opened up by the different techniques: the stiff formality of the early copper engravings, the meticulous detail possible with the steel engraving, the sketch-like spontaneity of the etching, the richness of the mezzotint with the effect of an oil-painting, the aquatint, often hand-coloured and excellent for reproducing watercolours, the grainy effect of lithography resembling a pencil or crayon drawing. The engraver's craft should not be seen as inferior to the creativity of the artist. Both contribute equally to an end product which, at its best, combines an aesthetically pleasing result with a mass-produced article. In looking through this volume the reader will embark on a journey which is not simply an historical odyssey but also a voyage of artistic discovery.

*Ian Maxted*
*Devon County Local Studies Librarian*

# Introduction

A city's history can be told through the images made of its topography, particularly by using those which show its buildings. These depictions, in whatever format, whether painted, drawn, printed or photographed, are invaluable as pictorial records of buildings which do not survive but the images themselves can tell us other things about the past. We need to consider why they were made: some were created to celebrate buildings which subsequent generations overlook or disregard. Few people today stop to admire the Brock Building at the junction of Fore Street with North Street but at the time it was constructed, in the 1880s, it was a structure Exeter was proud of. The lithograph made of it in 1884 is a reminder of its former place in society's self-estimation. But images in general tell us much more; while the 'Built Environment' is itself a legacy of former times, so too are the images made of them. They inform subsequent generations not merely about the buildings but also of the previous generations which created them.

## Selection of images

This is a book primarily of engravings but not exclusively so. Other mediums are included, notably lithographs, but a few others have been selected for which it has not been possible to specify how they were originally produced, particularly some made in the later nineteenth century. Some of these additional images help to place the engravings within the wider context of print-making. The choice of subject has been made more easily: they are limited to topographical images of non-religious buildings within the ancient city walls or immediately outside of them. Volume Two will comprise images of the cathedral and of the parish churches and chapels. Other types of engravings have been omitted from this collection including portraits of leading citizens, commercial letter heads and banknotes.[1] The first section in this volume comprises general views of the city which help to place it within its geographical situation and see it more as a corporate whole. These are followed by five further sections on buildings along the river Exe, the castle and gates, public buildings, the streets and townhouses along with Northernhay, and the last section relates to two events in the city's history which produced a

THE EXETER PIE MAN.

*An atypical portrait of an Exeter citizen (Devon & Exeter Institution, no reference number)*

ÆSOP'S FABLES ILLUSTRATED.

*Exeter's statue of St Peter as used in a nineteenth-century local parody*

*(Westcountry Studies Library, OPr)*

number of interesting engravings. The earliest image was taken from a drawing made of the city in the middle of the seventeenth century and the latest shows the High Street in 1942, just before the destruction which took place in the Second World War.

The majority of images are derived from the collection of the Devon County Library Service held at the Westcountry Studies Library with some additional ones taken from the Devon & Exeter Institution and the Royal Albert Memorial Museum. They have been selected from a larger body of illustrations and the criterion for inclusion has been to aim for a wide number and variety of buildings as well as to show the range of artistic and technical ability, and, in some cases, the accuracy in depicting the image. For example, Francis Jukes' aquatints of the East Gate have been selected partly because they are thought to the most accurate images whereas several later works have been omitted which are derivative of his work. Obviously, the choice of illustration is limited to what images have survived. While Exeter is fortunate in having these three establishments with extensive collections, irrespective of those images which suffered by the unfortunate practice of libraries in the early twentieth century (see Illustration 12 for a title written across it, Illustration 94 for stamping through the engraving), it is unknown how many other images survive unknown in private hands or in public collections far from Devon.

It is clearly important to include images of buildings that have not survived, even though their accuracy cannot be guaranteed. Some engravers may not have visited the city; it is difficult to understand how anyone who has been to Exeter can reposition the cathedral's west front onto the south tower and it is likely that this was an oversight caused by unfamiliarity rather than a deliberate act. This contrasts with a mezzotint by George S. Sanders (Illustration 59) in which he deliberately altered the character of Exeter by depicting Rougemont Tower in a rural setting, cattle are being herded apparently onto some unseen high pasture and an owl flies out from the tower. Moreover it redefines the subject's character by implying a legend with the title 'The Haunted Tower'. Also, it would be interesting to know the location of the 'Roman tower in the walls of Exeter', if it ever was in the city (Illustration 53), and the reliability of Illustration 54 as a view of Rougemont Castle particularly must be questioned. Interestingly, Illustration 7 was engraved more than 150 years after it was drawn and yet it may be more accurate than some of the later views engraved by men who never saw the actual building.

Other views are included precisely because they are not recognizable representations of locations as we know them. The etching of Mary Arches Street is hard to place today (Illustration 144) and two views of the Longbrook Valley (Illustrations 106 & 107) show it has altered beyond recognition from the middle of the nineteenth century. The images serve to remind later generations of architectural treasures which once enriched the life of Exeter but are now lost. Features such as the statue of Neptune atop the Public Baths, the clay ridge tile of the Equestrian on the roof of the Chevalier House in Fore Street and the statue of St Peter which stood at the corners of North and High Streets helped to define the city of Exeter. Likewise, the wood carvings in King John's Tavern were particularly expressive of Exeter and it would be interesting to know more of them: they were removed and put into storage in the nineteenth century but has the wood been incorporated into another building far from the city?

# Reasons for creating images

The selection has been made as comprehensive as possible, partly so that the many gaps and omissions in this record of the city's buildings may be seen in themselves significant: many buildings in the city were never engraved, drawn or painted. This poses the question as to why images were originally made. Initially they generally accompanied text: in the sixteenth and seventeenth centuries woodcuts were used to increase the sales of broadsides and were constantly recycled to illustrate ballads with vastly different subject matter. The increase in the number of books printed in the late eighteenth century created a demand for accompanying illustrations and these were, as they still are, cut out from the bindings and used as images in their own right. But increasingly engravings were not merely embellishments but legitimate consumer goods. This was partly due to the rise of domestic tourism in the late eighteenth century creating a demand for topographical prints as souvenirs. No doubt this is the cause for the cathedral being the most commonly engraved image of Exeter. These images of the cathedral, and of many other views of the city, were intended for the private homes of tourists as well as for those of local residents. Many of the other images of Exeter made in the later nineteenth century, and particularly in the early twentieth century, were of Elizabethan townhouses. These images increasingly became more popular and saleable: possibly the late Victorian sense of romanticism overtook the earlier association these buildings had with infectious disease; the generations which experienced cholera did not want engravings on their walls which reminded them of illness and squalor. But, once the threat of disease had passed, their descendents were able to enthuse about the 'old world charm' of these very same buildings.

Some prints were made not merely as souvenirs but to raise funds; when the Devon & Exeter Central School was being built in 1850 a lithograph was sold at the 'Fancy Sale' to help funding (Illustration 128). Others were produced to celebrate buildings as achievements: many such engravings appeared in *The Builder* as a celebration of Victorian architecture and as an advertisement for the architects. Engravings of banks and hotels made the public more aware of the buildings and often presented a sense of financial soundness, security, pride and moreover, corporate identity.

The extent to which the city gates were constantly engraved once their demolition had taken place is particularly interesting. The images were salvaged from the past, became iconic and recycled by subsequent generations irrespective of the accuracy of the original artist. Francis Jukes' views of the East Gate were made at the instigation of the City Council: in 1784 council members ordered that the gates were to be drawn as a permanent record of them. They gave John Hayman, who made the initial drawing, five guineas 'for his trouble' and a further five guineas towards his expenses in preparing the engravings. The gates, which had become impediments to traffic, were nevertheless a valued symbol of the city's identity.

Finally, images were created to accompany news reports, occasionally in local newspapers but more commonly by *The Illustrated London News*. The high costs of images restricted their use

*An Exeter Traders' Device, 1808 (Westcountry Studies Library, MPr/P&D08110)*

largely to national publications with long print runs and only occasionally did local papers use them.

Most of the images were sold with the expectation that they would be kept but others, notably those in newspapers and in *The Illustrated London News,* were more disposable. This may seem difficult to understand when a comparison is made between them and some locally produced engravings: many of the former have a greater attention to detail and higher degree of quality but the number of copies sold of national magazines made it financially possible to produce superior, if short-lived, images.

Many views were the result of newsworthy events such as national elections, the opening of the museum, the unveiling of statues, the Horticultural Exhibition in 1840, the bread riot of 1854, the launching of the *City of Exeter* in 1866, the visit of the British Association in 1869 and the burning of Exeter's theatre in 1887. But two events produced an extraordinary number of images which reflect the importance or interest in them to Exeter. The first was the cholera epidemic of 1832. No less than twenty engravings were produced to accompany Thomas Shapter's history of the disease in Exeter. The outbreak had a tremendous effect on the city as is seen by an examination of the engravings. The effect of the second event was less dramatic but, in stark contrast, a positive one. In 1850 the Royal Agricultural Society Exhibition was held in Exeter and some thirty illustrations were published to commemorate the event. The city rose to the occasion and the engravings demonstrate that it decorated itself in a manner that has not been matched in the 150 years since.

In this collection individual structures are nearly all more important than spaces and environments, even when, as is the case with the city gates, the structure's primary function is to define a given space. There are some exceptions: there are a great many general views which attempt to portray the city's collective identity while the river and High Street are depicted as avenues of commerce. Volume Two, with its religious buildings and concentration on the Cathedral, will provide altogether different pictorial approaches to the city.

## Topographical prints: the techniques and their significance

The creation of the images has been largely determined by technological advances and over the last five hundred years a number of different processes have been used. All engravings are made through a cutting process in which the image is created either in relief or intaglio. The earliest prints were made from wood blocks but were superseded in the eighteenth century by the use of copper plates either through line-engraving (cutting the design into the plate) or by etching (applying acid to cut the image into the plate). Images from copper plates were initially too expensive for all but high-quality books but an increasing population and growing market for books and prints at the end of the eighteenth century made it a medium more financially viable than woodcuts. Larger print runs and a demand for higher quality images reduced the demand for woodcuts. However, these prints made from copper plates were not sympathetic to the complexities of landscapes and an advancement was made with the discovery of the aquatint process which allowed for more shading and a greater subtlety. Aquatints, a form of etching in which a finer texture is achieved by burning areas instead of individual lines, became popular from the 1780s through to about 1830. At about that date two further developments took over for nearly a generation. Engravings began to be made from steel plates partly for commercial reasons: the harder surface of steel allowed for a greater print run which made it a more profitable process. At the same time lithographs became popular: in contrast to engravings this involved drawing with greasy ink on stone and creating an image from the untouched parts of the stone. These two processes dominated the mass-production of illustrations until the advent of photography in the 1870s. Thereafter engravings were self-conscious revivals of earlier outdated styles.

Three other processes are included in this book. In the very late eighteenth century wood began to reappear as a relief image carrier. Previously woodcuts were made from either blocks or planks of wood but the image was restricted, heavy and crude. By the early nineteenth century wood engravings were a major medium for illustrating books and such newspapers as *The Illustrated London News*. This involved using fine or hard-grained woods such as boxwood and cutting across the grain of the block or blocks joined together. The result was a more sophisticated and commercially viable image given that the process allowed a larger number of copies to be printed. Interestingly, the images were often of news stories and were dependent upon artists quickly depicting the event and then engravers producing the blocks in very short periods of time. A late nineteenth century movement revived the earlier woodcuts but this was a conscious effort and used partly to signify a sense of old England. Yet another process used was the linocut. As a softer medium, linoleum has been used in a similar way to creating woodcuts but is not suitable for very long runs of printing. Two examples (Illustrations 148 & 153) appear in this book. Finally, one example of a mezzotint has been included (Illustration 59). This process involved rocking the entire surface to create a background of fine black points into which the image would be cut.[2]

## The engravers and artists

More than 85 individuals were responsible for the images in this book. Generally the engraver is indicated to the right of the illustration mostly by either *sculpsit*, *sculp*. or *sc*. (engraved) or *fecit.*, *fec.*, *fe.*, *ft.*, or even *f*. (made). The original artist who drew the view is noted on the left generally by either *delineavit* or *del*. (designed). In other cases the individuals remain anonymous and in others one individual is given credit for being both artist and engraver/lithographer.

They include a number of national and local figures, notably N.H.J. Baird (1854–1936), etcher who lived in Topsham; Samuel Buck (1696–1779), draughtsman and engraver, who produced illustrations of England and Wales, and his brother Nathaniel Buck; George Bryant Campion (1796–1870), lithographer and watercolourist, who was a drawing master at the Military School, Woolwich; T.E. Chapman, lithographer and professor of drawing, who lived in Sidwell Street and Verney Place; William Davey (1818–*c*.90), produced line engravings, lithographs, mezzotints and stipple engravings; William Deeble, a painter who also produced line and steel engravings; Joseph Farington (1747–1821), landscape painter, visited Devon twice during 1809 and 1810 partly to illustrate Daniel and Samuel Lysons' *Magna Britannia: Devon*; William Gauci, lithographer, son of Maxim Gauci (1774–1854), who worked in London; John Greig, steel engraver, etcher and lithographer, who worked with J.S. Storer on antiquarian and topographical works; Charles Joseph Hullmandel (1789–1850), lithographer who has been credited with introducing the use of graduated tints and white in highlights as well as inventing lithotints; Thomas Jeavons (d.1867), line and steel engraver; Frederick Christian Lewis (1779–1856), worked in aquatints, etchings, mezzotints and steel, line and stipple engravings; Frederick Nash (1782–1856), who produced aquatints and lithographs as well as paintings; Thomas Abiel Prior (1809–1886), who produced line and steel engravings as well as mezzotints; George S. Sanders (1810–76), produced line engravings and mezzotints; Thomas Hosner Shepherd, steel-engraver, water-colourist and draughtsman; Francis Stevens (1781–1823), etcher and watercolourist, may have been a native of Exeter; Henry Sargant Storer (1795–1837), line engraver and draughtsman, exhibited at the Royal Academy and worked with his father James Sargant Storer (1771–1853), line engraver and draughtsman; Henry Wallis (c.1805–1890), line and steel engraver, and brother of Robert and William; and William Woolnoth, steel engraver and brother of Thomas.[3]

Undoubtedly, the most famous artist was J.M.W. Turner but the majority are much less known and many of the illustrations are anonymous. Only five women can be identified: these were Letitia Byrne (1779–1849), an etcher who also produced steel engravings, Mrs George Rowe who worked with her husband; Frances Margery Hayman, Primrose Pitman and Nella Delves were all involved with the Exeter School of Art in the 1920s and produced particularly atmospheric depictions of the city. Other local people of interest were Charles Frederick Williams (1810–94), who lived in Palace Street, and Thomas Hewitt Williams, lithographer, landscape artist and portrait painter who was interested in the picturesque. He lived in the High Street.

Five local men were particularly active in the creation of images of Exeter. These were Henry Beasley, John Gendall, George Rowe, William Spreat and George Townsend. Henry Beasley, printer, worked at premises in North Street where he published *The Devon Chronicle* and a number of views of the city. Among his works were *The Exeter Guide and Itinerary* (1836) and *Views in Devonshire* (1848–71). John Gendall (1790–1865), a distinguished water-colourist who was nevertheless described in 1856 as 'carver, gilder and printseller', lived in Exeter including on the High Street and Cathedral Yard and among his works are the series of views depicting the cholera outbreak in 1832. His work included *Etched Views of Exeter* (1834). George Rowe (1796–1864), lithographer and painter, was born in Exeter. He worked from about the age of thirty either from his home in Mount Radford or in premises in Sidwell Street. Rowe later moved to Cheltenham before emigrating to the Australian gold-fields and subsequently returning to Exeter where he died. Among his works were *Views of Exeter* (c.1828), *Forty-eight Views of Cottages and Scenery at Sidmouth, Devon* (1826), *Views upon the river Dart, Devonshire* (c.1826) and *The Beauties of the North of Devon* (c.1828). William Spreat (?1806–c.76), lithographer, worked in premises in Gandy Street, High Street and Castle Street. He produced at least two hundred lithographs. In 1853 he gave lithographs of Exeter as gifts to his customers. He had intended to emigrate to Ireland in 1845 but stayed in Exeter where he went bankrupt in 1869. Among his work were *A Description of the county of Devonshire* (c.1840) and *Picturesque Sketches of the Churches of Devon* (1842). George Townsend (1813–1894), who styled himself 'artist, lithographer and drawing master', was based in the High Street and lived in Deanery Place. Among his works were the two series of *Views in Devonshire* (1848–71, 1853–c.75).

### Leaves from a Sketch-Book.

#### THE CITY OF EXETER.

The meetings, begun this week, of the British Association for the Advancement of Science in the city of Exeter, have induced us to prepare, for our Journal of this date, a General View of that pleasant capital of Devonshire, with a few examples of the antique and picturesque bits of architecture to be found in its public buildings and streets. The situation of Exeter, covering the westerly slope of a broad hill declining to the green valley of the Exe, about ten miles from the sea, and looking towards the lofty range of Haldon, and the distant heights of Dartmoor, is salubrious and agreeable. It is 173 miles from London by the old coach road, 193 miles by the Great Western Railway through Bristol, and 171 miles by the London and South-Western line, through Salisbury and Honiton, which follows the ancient route to the west of England. The population of Exeter is still nearly forty thousand; since the loss of its maritime commerce, which was chiefly with Spain and Portugal, with some coasting trade, and of its serge manufactures, which were, half a century ago, an export of considerable value, has been compensated by the residence here of many families of gentry, and by the increasing agricultural prosperity of Devon. No place in the west of England, after Bath and Clifton, which are more especially laid out for the attraction of visitors, is a more inviting abode for people desirous of provincial retirement with the enjoyments of good society and of cheerful scenery, the soothing influence of a mild climate, and many interesting features of the neighbourhood. The favourite seaside watering-places within a short journey—Sidmouth, Exmouth, Teignmouth, and Torquay, on the south coast; Ilfracombe, Lynmouth, and Westward Ho, on the north coast of Devon, besides many others not less beautiful, though less generally known—are yearly frequented by greater numbers in search of the pure-more waters of the ocean. A more bracing and invigorating atmosphere than that of the South Devon coast is breathed in the upland villages of Dartmoor, lately made accessible by a railway; and the singularly wild landscape of that region, consisting of a vast hillowy expanse of heather or turf, rising into bold brown hills, everywhere broken

WESTGATE QUARTER.

or crested with innumerable protruding rocks of sparkling granite, and cleft by torrents fringed with stunted oaks or feathery larches, have something of a mountain character. The valley of the Exe, however, like the rest of the fertile parts of Devonshire, which contains no tract of level country, but is full of low swelling hills, presents an aspect of softness, richness, and freshness of verdure, unequalled by any district of Great Britain in a more easterly longitude. With pasture and meadow grounds of wonderful luxuriance, the massive earthen hedges around the small fields are usually topped with rows of mighty elms, spreading their leafy branches wide, and giving a sylvan appearance to the landscape. The deep red colour of the soil, and of many of the buildings, affords a pleasing relief to the profusion of deep green, while the prospect is adorned by the stately mansions and well-wooded parks of several county magnates. From the hill called Marypolehead, a mile northward of Exeter, the spectator has a noble view of the lower valley of the Exe, down to Topsham, and of its spacious estuary, which is an arm of the sea two miles wide, terminating with the red sandstone cliffs of Dawlish. Our Artist has chosen a different point of view, from the Cowick Hills to the west of the city, above the opposite bank of the river, from which the face of the city is more directly seen; and in the large Engraving, which occupies

OLD HOUSES, NORTH-STREET.

ROUGEMONT CASTLE.

OLD HOUSES, FORE-STREET.

GUILDHALL.

*A page of wood engravings depicting Exeter from* The Illustrated London News

(The Illustrated London News, *21 August 1869*)

# Conclusion

In 1869 *The Illustrated London News* published a page of views of Exeter. The reporter noted of one of the illustrations, entitled the 'Westgate quarter', that it was:

*Scarcely likely to attract the notice of visitors . . . There are many quaint-looking old houses, with gabled roofs to the street and with jutting wooden fronts – there are heavy stone arches; grotesque figures, sculptured or painted; winding alleys and secluded courts, with the long back gardens in the rear of the tradesmen's houses and shops which show the old-fashioned character of the city . . .*

This description of the West Quarter may not have appealed to Victorians but the modern reader is more likely to reflect upon the subsequent destruction of this area in the Second World War as well as that which occurred in the immediate years afterwards in a spirit of 'improvement'. Later generations are more likely to be enticed, and frustrated, by the depiction. The changing attitudes expressed by it is a reminder of how useful and stimulating engravings and other images are: they help us not only remember the previous generations who created the built environment but hopefully open up new opportunities in allowing us to re-examine those buildings we are already familiar with and introduce buildings yet unknown.

[1] For banknotes see John Ryton, *Banks and Banknotes of Exeter, 1769–1906* (Exeter, 1983).

[2] A useful history of printing is provided by Raymond Lister, *Prints and Printmaking: A Dictionary and Handbook of the Art in Nineteenth-century Britain* (1984).

[3] J.V. Somers Cocks, *Devon Topographical Prints, 1660–1870 – A Catalogue and Guide* (Exeter, 1977); Lister, *Prints and Printmaking*; Sam Smiles and Michael Pidgley, *The Perfection of England* (Exeter, 1995); Devon & Exeter Institution, index of Devon artists by Samuel Smiles.

# General Views

*Excester or Exceter is a famous and an ancient city being the Metropole and Emporium of the west parts of England and situated and lyeing in the province called sometimes Danmonia that is to say the country of valleys for whereas [there] are many hills (as that country is full of hills and mountains) there are many valleys. But now corruptly it is named Devonia or Devonshire.*

JOHN HOOKER ALIAS VOWELL, *THE DESCRIPTION OF THE CITY OF EXETER*, C.1600

*1    Copper line engraving by & after S. & N. Buck, 1736. A panorama view of the city from the west
with St David's church and Rougemont to the top left. The Workhouse is shown to the left of the
cathedral and the tower of St Thomas' church to the far right.*

2   *Copper line engraving by & after S. & N. Buck, 1736. A second view from the south west. It depicts St Thomas' church nearly in the middle with St Mary Major church above and to the left, and Bowhay House is in the bottom left-hand corner. The bridge, seen in the previous view, is obscured by the village of St Thomas.*

*3   Copper line engraving after William Stukeley, 1723, viewed from the west bank of the river Exe. Stukeley made the drawing while on a visit that year and wrote the bridge 'is of great length and has houses on both sides and both ends. A considerable void space in the middle; there is a church upon it with a tower steeple.'*

4   *Copper line engraving by & after J. Ryland, c.1750, viewed from the west with the church tower of St Thomas aligned with the Cathedral.*

5    *Anonymous copper line engraving, 1771, with the city again viewed from the west.*

6    *Anonymous copper line engraving, after Ryland, c.1775, with only slight differences from the earlier views.*

7   *Anonymous aquatint, 1821, which was produced to illustrate* The Travels of Cosmo the Third.
*The Grand Duke of Tuscany visited Exeter as part of his tour of England in 1669 and the illustration
was 'delineated at that period by artists in the suite of Cosmos'. It views the city from the Longbrook
valley prominently showing the castle, walls, cathedral and St Mary Major church. The original
drawings remain in Italy.*

8    *Lithograph by & after T. E. Chapman, 1825, of Exeter viewed from St Thomas probably along Alphington Street.*

9    *Etching by F. C. Lewis after a sketch by F. Stevens, 1827, with the walls prominently shown.*

10   *Etching by F. C. Lewis after F. Stevens, 1827, viewed from St Thomas.*

11    *Etching by & after T.H. Williams, 1830, viewed from near Whitestone and Exwick. Williams wrote in his tour of Exeter that this was 'the finest view of the city and river as a whole'.*

12    *Anonymous wood engraving, 1850, showing the newly-built railway station at St Davids. The*
*illustration was printed in a newspaper in early July 1850, probably to accompany a report on the*
*agricultural exhibition then in Exeter. See Illustration 222.*

*13    Steel line engraving by William Le Petit after W. H. Bartlett, 1829.*

14 *Wood engraving by I. Read, 1869. The meeting of the British Association for the Advancement of Science during the summer of 1869 at Exeter prompted a report and this illustration in* The Illustrated London News. *It noted that the city's situation was 'salubrious and agreeable' and that no place west of Bath or Clifton was a 'more inviting abode for people desirous of provincial retirement'.*

15    *Steel line engraving by T. A. Prior after W. Harvey, 1849, of the city viewed from Cowley with an idyllic rural scene in the forefront and Exeter at the end of the rainbow.*

16   *Steel line engraved vignette after G. Townsend, c.1848, with the new railway prominently shown.*

17   *Anonymous steel line engraved vignette, c.1860, of the city viewed from Exwick with a train along the tracks.*

19   *Steel line engraved vignette by Newman & Co., c.1845.*

18   *Anonymous steel line engraving, c.1830.*

20   *Anonymous steel line engraved vignette, 1854.*

21    *Wood engraving by H. Fenn after Robert Paterson, c.1880, of the city from Exwick.*

22   Lithograph by George Rowe, c.1826-30, entitled 'Exeter, from Cowick Hill'
dedicated to Samuel Trehawke Kekewich, Exeter Member of Parliament. Fore Street is
prominently shown as is Pennsylvania Park.

23  *Lithograph by W. Gauci after C. F. Williams, c.1835, viewed from Heavitree.*

24   *Lithograph by & after W. Spreat, c.1845, viewed from Union Road.*

*25   Lithograph by & after G. Rowe, c.1828, viewed from Pennsylvania Road with the tower of St Sidwell's church to the left.*

*26    Steel line engraving by William Le Petit after T. Allom, 1831, viewed from Pennsylvania Road*

*27    Steel line engraving by J. Henshall after G. B. Campion, 1832, viewed from Pennsylvania Road.*

*28    Lithograph vignette by & after G. Rowe, c.1835.*

*29    Steel line engraved vignette after G. Townsend, c.1850, looking towards the south-east.*

30    *Anonymous steel line engraved vignette, 1846, with the tower of St Sidwell's church in the*

*right hand corner.*

## The River Exe, bridge and quay

*The River X is a fine stream; they have made several bays or weirs above the bridge, which casts the water into many channels for the conveniences of turning all their mills, by which means they have composed a little island, for at the end it again returns into its own united channel.*

CELIA FIENNES, 1698

31   *Lithograph by George Townsend, 1860, viewing the quay from the canal showing*

*Colleton Crescent*

*32    Copper line engraving by J. Storer after Brockedon, 1811*

*33    Anonymous steel line engraved vignette, c.1855, of Trew's Weir.*

*34   Steel line engraving by A. Carse after T. Allom, 1831*

*35   An anonymous engraving, 1840*

*36    Copper line engraving by J. & H. S. Storer after J. André, 1823*

*37    Lithograph by George Rowe, looking from the Ship Canal towards Colleton Crescent, 1828*

*38  Steel line engraving by T. Jeavons after J. M. W. Turner, 1829*

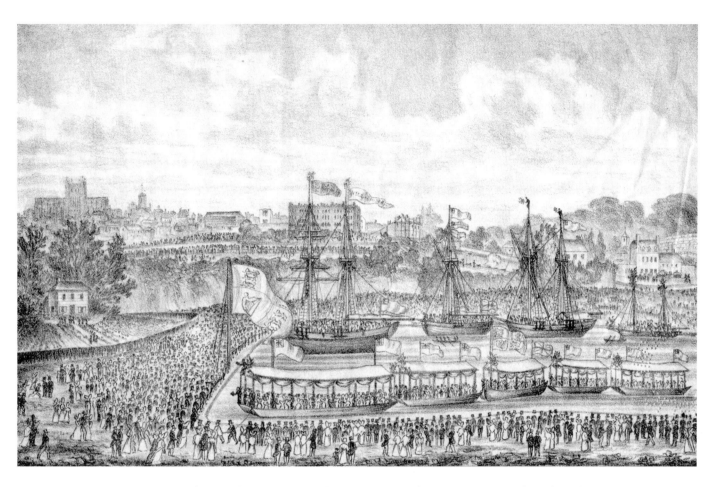

39    Lithograph by J. Roberts, 1830, entitled 'Opening the New Bason at Exeter, September 29th 1830'.
*The works were under the supervision of James Green.* The Exeter Flying Post *reported that the city
had a 'holiday appearance' and that five barges processed up the canal to the city: on the first boat were
leading politicians and gentlemen, on the second were musicians who played throughout the day, and
the last three boats held nearly 300 gentlemen and tradesmen. After the thousands of local people
watched the ceremonies a civic dinner was held at the Royal Public Rooms.*

*40   Lithograph by W. Gauci after C. F. Williams, c.1835*

41 *Lithograph by & after W. Spreat, c.1855, with the Custom House to the right*

Exeter had a stone bridge by the end of the twelfth century but the Medieval bridge, which now lies in ruins and encircled by a steady line of traffic, stretched at least 700 feet from the West Gate across marshland and the river Exe to St Thomas. It was replaced in the late eighteenth century and several other bridges were later built at the same crossing point. Also see Illustrations 4 and 216.

*42   An anonymous engraving, c.1800*

*43   Wood engraving by A. Jenkins after J. Coggan, 1806*

*44   Steel line engraving by C. J. G. Sprake, 1831, of a replacement bridge.*

*45–7   First of three etchings by F.C. Lewis after F. Stevens, 1827, of views of the river and bridges.*

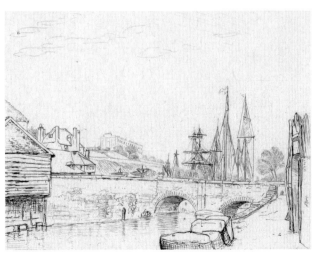

48    *Lithograph by G. Townsend, c.1850, showing Exe Island from Exe Bridge*

49    *Wood engraving by an unidentified resident of St David's, 1856, of the Port Royal Inn.* The
Illustrated London News *reported on 14 September 1856 that on the afternoon of 7 September a
whirlwind descended upon the inn and lifted a four-oared gig some fifteen feet into the air.*

*50  Anonymous etching possibly by J. Gendall, 1834, of the quay bridge near Cricklepit Mills.*

## The Castle and Gates

*It is pleasantly seated upon a hill, amongst hills, saving towards the sea, very beautiful in building, and for quantity, matchable with most cities, which was first encompassed with a wall of stone by King Athelstane, in a manner circular, and beautified with battlements, and many turrets interposed, being before enclosed only with a ditch and fortified with stakes… This city hath six gates, the compass of whose wall's measure, is a mile and an half…*

TRISTRAM RISDON, *THE CHOROGRAPHICAL DESCRIPTION OR SURVEY OF THE COUNTY OF DEVON*,

EARLY SEVENTEENTH CENTURY

51   *Copper line engraving by R. White, 1744, showing 'Athelstan's Tower' to the right and promenading along Northernhay*

Rougemont Castle, the Red Hill, was begun by the Normans shortly after the Conquest. The oval-shaped building replaced an earlier fortification which was situated in the West Quarter overlooking the river. Two circles of ditches originally enclosed the castle buildings which relied upon the sheer drop of between twenty and thirty feet for protection. Height was increased through artificial building and by quarrying the cliff face for building materials. The castle served as the centre of the Royal power in the city for centuries, became enmeshed with the Duchy of Cornwall and was later the seat of the Devon County Council from its formation in the later nineteenth century until it moved to County Hall on Topsham Road in the early 1960s.

*52    Anonymous etching 'entitled view of the sally port to the castle of Exeter', 1771*

The sally port, on the Northernhay side of the castle, is shown before its ruined state
(as on the previous page).

*53    Wood engraving by Mason, 1850, of the 'Roman' Tower possibly at Exeter.*

54    *Line engraving taken from a drawing made from a painting on a clock by Jacob Lovelace in the*
*early eighteenth century. It would be interesting to know what image the painting itself was based on*
*but it is questionable whether it depicts Rougemont Castle. The clock, along with its painting, was*
*vandalised in the second world war and its remains are now in the Royal Albert Memorial Museum.*

55   *Anonymous wood engraved vignette, 1836. The Court House was built in 1774 to the design of*
*Philip Stowey and Thomas Jones but improved by James Wyatt.*

56   *Anonymous wood engraving entitled 'Inauguration of the Fortescue Memorial in the Castle Yard, Exeter'.* The Illustrated London News *on 19 September 1863 reported that the statue of Hugh, Earl Fortescue, was paid for through public subscription and executed in Sicilian marble by E.B. Stephens. The symbolism includes the grasping of his robe to indicate his rank in the peerage, left leg exhibiting his garter to show the honour bestowed on him by Victoria for his political service, the order of St Patrick around his neck is a reminder of his service in Ireland and his coat's collar and cuffs indicate his connection with the county as Lord Lieutenant. The statue is now situated on the west side of Castle Yard.*

*57    Engraving by F. Jukes after W. Davey, 1794, probably more accurate than the majority of later views.*

58    *Etching by Letitia Byrne after Joseph Farington, 1822, of the tower within the cultivated landscape at Edmund Granger's Rougemont House.*

*59   Mezzotint by & after G. S. Sanders, 1838. This unusual depiction of the 'haunted' tower, with its cattle, seems more in keeping with tales of Lydford than Exeter.*

*60   Copper line engraving by Sparrow, 1772, with Rougemont Tower and the castle gates to the right*

61  *Etching by T.H. Williams, 1806, in a picturesque fashion.*

62  *Anonymous lithograph of untitled view of the judges leaving the Assize Court headed by John*
   *Cook, Captain of the Sheriff's troop, mid nineteenth-century.*

63  *Etching by NHJ Baird, 1870s, showing the landscaped features around Athelstan's Tower approaching from Northernhay.*

64   *Anonymous copper line engraving, 1826. 'King Athelstan's palace' stood in Cary Street.*
*Alexander Jenkins wrote in 1806 that it 'was an ancient edifice built of hewn stone, consisting of*
*circular stone staircases, leading to many small vaulted rooms. This building, according to tradition,*
*was once the habitation of King Athelstan, termed by the vulgar King Addlestone's palace. It was*
*taken down some years ago and modern buildings erected on its site particularly large and*
*commodious wine vaults'.*

Exeter had five ancient gates in the city walls. The Water Gate, otherwise known as the Quay Gate, was cut in the city wall just above the quay in 1565 and removed in 1815. There may have been an earlier gate.

65   *Copper line engraving by F. Nash after Joseph Farington, published 1822 but drawn a decade before.*

*66    Etching by J.C. Griffiths, 1873*

*67    Etching by J.C. Griffiths, 1873*

*68    Steel line engraving by C. J. G. Sprake, 1831*

The North Gate, a medieval structure, was situated at the city end of where the Iron Bridge now stands. It was demolished in 1769, the first of the city's gates to be destroyed.

69  *Anonymous etching,1792*

70  *Steel line engraving by C. J. G. Sprake,*
*1831*

71  *Etching by J.C. Griffiths, 1873*

The West Gate was situated at the entrance to the city at Exe Bridge. Alexander Jenkins wrote
in 1806 that it was 'a very ancient but mean structure and inferior in point of architecture to
the other city gates. It consists of a square tower, something loftier than the walls, without any
projection on the outside or flanking bulwarks. In this tower is an ill-contrived room, with a
small window looking towards the suburbs. On the interior front are the remains of an
inscription now obliterated. The entrance into the city is through an irregular pointed arch,
and the whole has the appearance of remote antiquity; it has no insignia of arms or ornament
remaining on it, and being now in a very ruinous state, will, in all probability, be soon taken
down'. It was demolished nine years later in 1815.

The East Gate stood at the entrance to the city on the main road from London at what is now the juncture of the High Street and Sidwell Street.

It was demolished in 1784.

72   *First of two aquatints by F. Jukes after W. Davey, 20 October 1785. The view is looking towards Sidwell Street. The City commissioned these as a pictorial record for future generations.*

73    *Second aquatint by F. Jukes after W. Davey, 1785, looking into the city.*

74   *Copper line engraving by J. Smith after E. Dayes, 1803. One of many views of the gate.*

The Medieval South Gate held the ancient city prison comprising of two wings, one for felons and the other for debtors. Alexander Jenkins in 1806 thought it was 'a massy building of hewn stone'. He wrote that 'the entrance from the suburbs is through a lofty pointed arch flanked by circular towers. Over the gateway is a niche where lately stood a mutilated statue in a magisterial robe. This front is likewise decorated with angels supporting the Royal and City arms. The interior arch of the gateway from its semicircular form appears of Saxon construction and is probably some remains of the ancient gate, the present one being erected in the reign of Henry 7th'. He also noted that it was a prison and 'a worse one can hardly be imagined. The felons' prison is on the western side, consisting of three separate ground rooms, two of them appropriated for the men, and one for women. These rooms from their damp situation and darkness may not improperly be called dudgeons and to add to their miserable state, the common sewer and drain from Southernhay runs directly under them into which an opening being made for their own conveniences, a very noisome smell commonly arises. The Debtors' side, though not so bad as the Felons', is gloomy and unwholesome and confinement in it is too severe a punishment for those unhappy objects, whose crimes are, too often, only misfortunes and poverty. Over the felons' cells is a large room called the shoe, from the poor debtors begging the charity of passengers from the barred window, and to receive which, they let down an old shoe by a cord'. The gate was demolished thirteen years later in 1819.

75  *Copper line engraving by F. Nash after J. Farington, 1822. Farington made the drawing a decade earlier.*

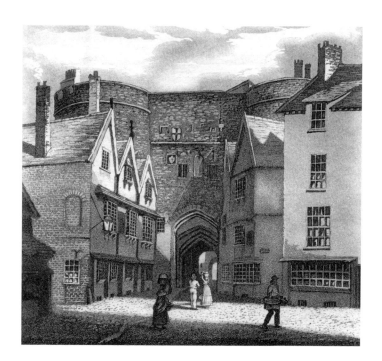

76  *Anonymous aquatint, c.1825, made after the gate was demolished.*

*77    Steel line engraving by C. J. G. Sprake, 1831*

*78    Etching by J.C. Griffiths, 1873 of the South Gate*

79    *Etching probably by J. Gendall, 1834, of the north side. Made after the South Gate*
*was demolished.*

*80    Another etching, probably by Gendall, 1834, of the gate's south side.*

The city had several more gates in addition to the five ancient ones to the city walls. In 1286 the Cathedral was enclosed with a series of gates, the most notable being the Broadgate which was demolished more than five hundred years later in 1825. It was situated at the north-west corner of Cathedral Close opening onto the High Street, the main route for ceremonial processions from the Guildhall through to the West Front of the Cathedral.

81 *Copper line engraving by F. Nash after J. Farington, 1822, of Broadgate from his drawing made a decade before.*

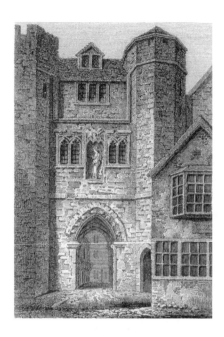

*82   Copper line engraving by J. Storer after*
*Brockedon, 1811.*

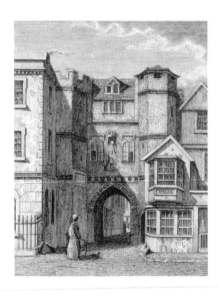

*83   Steel line engraving by C. J. G.*
*Sprake, 1831.*

*84   Etching by J.C. Griffiths, 1873.*

*85   Lithograph by C. Hullmandel after Isaac Bird, 1822.*

# The Public Buildings

*Exeter, a city famous for two things, which we seldom find united in the same town, viz. that tis full of gentry, and good company, and yet full of trade and manufactures also.*

DANIEL DEFOE, *A TOUR THROUGH THE WHOLE ISLAND OF GREAT BRITAIN*, 1724

86   *Anonymous lithograph, c.1830, showing the High Street devoid of traffic.*

Three nineteenth-century views of the High Street,
a topographical feature of the city long-commented on by visitors.

87    *Anonymous steel line engraved vignette, c.1860.*

88    *Steel line engraving after G. Townsend, 1853.*

89    *Anonymous steel line engraved vignette, 1876.*

90  *Copper line engraving by R. White, 1744, of the Guildhall made as an inset in Rocque's map of the city.*

The Guildhall is a medieval building with a late fifteenth-century core. The front, stretching out across the pavement on its granite columns, is a replacement of the 1590s. For hundreds of years the city's official meetings were held here and also judgements were passed by the city's magistrates on miscreants. Alexander Jenkins wrote in 1806 that it was 'a jumble of ancient and modern architecture but a later visitor, in the 1930s, remarked on the building being coloured like liver and bacon and particularly on the respect with which locals held it.

91  *Copper line engraving by J. & H. S. Storer after R. Brown, 1823.*

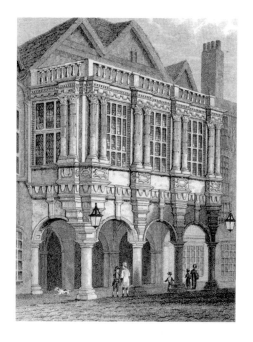

*92    Steel line engraving by W. Deeble after Baynes and Glennic, 1829.*

*93    Steel line engraving by J. Tingle after T. H. Shepherd, c.1845*

*94   Steel line engraving by William Le Petit after W. H. Bartlett, 1829/32*

*95   Lithograph possibly by W. Spreat, c.1840*

96   *Wood engraving entitled 'Bread Riot at Exeter' from* The Illustrated London News, *21 January 1854. A troop of the 3<sup>rd</sup> Light Dragoons are pictured stationed outside the Guildhall after a mob of mainly labourers' wives attacked bakers' shops in the city. It was reported that the women rioted after increases in the price of bread and that some bakers threw bread in order to appease the crowd. The police pursued rioters to Alphington and Exminster.*

97    *Etching by NHJ Baird, 1870s, looking west towards Fore Street*

*98   Etching by NHJ Baird, 1870s, of the interior of the Guildhall*

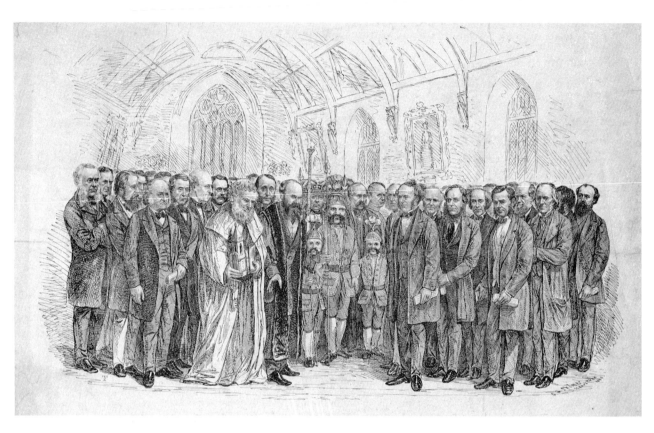

99    *Engraving by George Palmer after TF, 1896, which appears to have been printed with an etching. It depicts a reception at the Guild Hall for members of the British Association. According to notes written on the back of the engraving the men were, from left to right, William Kendall, either T.J. Bremond or J. Milford, Sir Stafford Northcote, John Drew or Rev. Richard Kirnam, Sir John Bowring, William Reginald, 11th Earl of Devon, Sir John Duke Coleridge, Edgar Bowring, figure of St Peter, Edward Andrew Sanders, Henry Samuel Ellis, Mace Sergeant Howard, son of Mathew the Miller, Mathew the Miller, William Dennis Moore, Mr Stere, son of Mathew the Miller, John Phillips, Sir George Gabriel Stokes (President of the British Association), William Pengelley, Sir Joseph Hooker, Dr Leon Levi, Professor Thomas Henry Huxley, Charles Darwin, Sir Richard Owen, possibly William Huggins, T. Archer Hirst. The meeting of the Association was timed to coincide with the opening of the Museum.*

100  *Anonymous wood engraving, November, 1868, of the interior of the Guidhall. It appeared in* The Illustrated London News *to depict the nomination for the election of that year.*

101 *Copper line engraving by R. White, 1744, which appears as an illustration to Rocque's map of the city. The City Hospital was founded with a bequest made in 1667 and situated on the lower end of Paris Street. It was built in the 1670s but surpassed by the Workhouse some forty years later. Not long afterwards, in the 1740s, another competitor was built: the Devon and Exeter Hospital was erected through the efforts of Dean Alured Clarke in Southernhay.*

102    Copper line engraving by R. White, 1744, which appears as an illustration to Rocque's map of
the city, of the north face of the Southernhay building.

103   *Copper line engraving by W. Woolnoth after W. Davey, c.1800, of the front of the hospital.*

104  *Copper line engraving of the front of the Devon & Exeter Hospital, 1752*

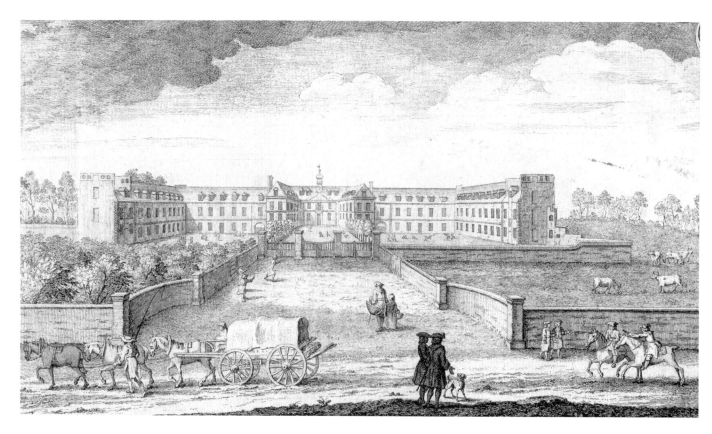

105    Copper line engraving by R. White, 1744, which appears as an illustration to Rocque's map of
the city. The Work House was built from 1700 to 1707 and run by the Exeter Corporation of the Poor.
It was situated on Heavitree Road on the site now managed by the National Health Service. The
buildings were largely destroyed in 1942 with a portion saved which formed part of Exeter City
Hospital now part of the complex of the Royal Devon & Exeter Healthcare NHS Trust.

106    *Steel line engraving by William Le Petit after Thomas Allom, 1831. The former church of St David's can be seen in the distance.*

The Longbrook Valley before the coming of the railway. The House of Correction was situated on the north side of the city and built from 1807 to 1809. It was replaced in the 1850s by Devon County Prison (on the same site).

*107    Steel line engraving by H. Wallis after G. B. Campion, 1832.*

*108   Wood engaving by A. Jenkins after J.*
*Hayman, 1770*

*109   Anonymous engraving, 1770*

*110   Steel line engraving by C. J. G. Sprake,*
*1831*

The Great Conduit, or Carfaix, was situated at the corner of Fore Street and South Street. In
1770, after more than three hundred years of supplying Exeter with water, it was demolished
to improve the flow of traffic. According to Jenkins in 1806 it was decorated with weather
vanes on the pinnacles at the four corners, there were niches in the east and west fronts with
mutilated statues, two lions and two unicorns stood on the corners of the architrave and there
were decorations of cherubin and armorial bearings.

*111    Lithograph by W. Hackett, c.1830, of the replacement conduit in South Street. See Illustration 201.*

*112    Steel line engraving by & after C. J. G. Sprake, 1831*

113    *Lithograph by H. Besley and Son, 1850*

114    *Steel line engraving by J. F. Lambert after W. H. Bartlett, 1830. The Baths were built in Southernhay Square in 1821 and demolished in 1868. Neptune stood guard over the main entrance.*

*115   Anonymous aquatint, 1804*

Exeter has had a succession of theatres. The second one is depicted here when newly built in
1804 between Southernhay and Bedford Circus. In 1806 Alexander Jenkins described it as 'a
neat and convenient theatre of brick, with stone copings. In the front is a colonnade,
supported by Tuscan columns, and over the colonnade is a stone escutcheon on which are
carved in relief the city arms'. It was destroyed by fire in 1820.

*116 Anonymous wood engraving, 1887, which appeared in* The Illustrated London News *and* The Western Times.

The fourth theatre, the Theatre Royal, was built in 1886 at the top of Longbrook Street and caught fire the following year on 5 September. The deaths of nearly two hundred patrons led to the insertion of fire screens in theatres. *The Exeter Flying Post* reported that as 'numerous and disastrous have been the fires in Exeter, there has never been one to equal that which occurred in the Theatre Royal'. The building was demolished in 1963.

117    *Anonymous half tone reproduction from a drawing, 1887.*

118    *Anonymous half tone reproduction from a wood engraving, 1887.*

*119   Wood engraving by W.E. Hockin after B. Sly of the proposed plan for the museum.*

The Royal Albert Memorial Museum was built from 1865 to 1866 to a design by John Hayward. His original plan for a tall central tower was modified with the insertion of a rose window. The use of different-coloured stone remains a distinguishing feature in the city.

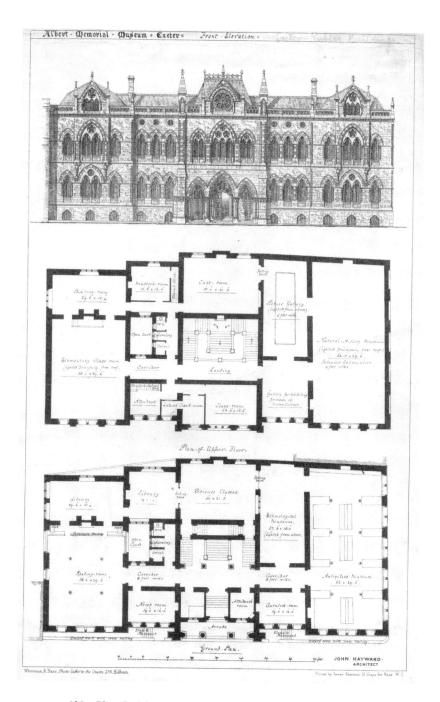

120   *Plans by John Hayward for the front elevation of the museum.*

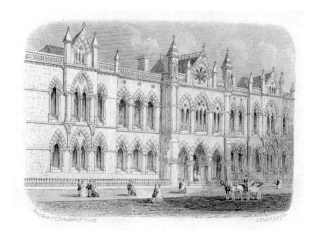

121  *Anonymous steel line engraved vignette, 1876.*

122  *Steel line engraved vignette after C. King, 1871.*

123    *Lithograph possibly by W. Spreat, c.1850. The Post Office was based from 1850 in this building in Queen Street for more than a dozen years. Queen Street was laid out in the 1830s, named in honour of Queen Victoria, to cross the steep Longbrook Valley. It removed from the city a cluster of buildings associated with the cholera epidemic of 1832. See Illustration 247.*

124   *Anonymous wood engraving, 1866, from* The Illustrated London News. *The* City of Exeter
*was launched on the first of October 1866 before a crowd of many thousands. The boat, 34 feet long
and just over 8 feet wide, had arrived several days before at Central Station. It was hoisted upon a
carriage and drawn by eight horses through the city in a public procession headed by the mayor. A
crew of Exmouth coastguardsmen, dressed in their cork jackets, accompanied the vessel as did,
amongst many others, a temperance fife and drum band and four fire brigades. It was reported that
although Exeter was 'far enough from the coast to make the sight of a lifeboat a novelty, yet near
enough to know something of the danger from which the vessel of mercy is intended to save our
sailors'. The vessel was sent to Brixham.*

125 *Wood engraving by I. Read, 1869.* The Illustrated London News, *reported on 19 April 1869 that during Easter Week in 1869 the city raised funds for the Royal National Life-boat Institution. The Exmouth and Budleigh Salterton lifeboat was drawn on a carriage and processed through High Street, Sidwell Street, Southernhay and Fore Street before arriving at Northernhay Place. The illustration shows the boat being carried on Queen Street with the museum on the right.*

St John's Hospital, later St John's Hospital School, was situated on the High Street near the East Gate and operated as a school after the Reformation. It housed the Exeter Free Grammar School until 1840.

*126    Etching by R. Hancock after G. Moneypenny, 1760.*

127    *Lithograph by & after Stevens, 1824, of the gateway to St John's Hospital.*

128    *Lithograph by & after W. Spreat, c.1850. The Devon and Exeter Central School was built to a plan by G.W. Cumming, architect, in 1850 near Coombe Street and demolished in 1978.*

129   *Engraving by George Townsend, 1868. The National School was located in Bartholomew Street West near The Mint. The building is now a block of flats.*

130    Wood engraving by Jewett & Co. after a drawing by H.T. Keques, 1870, with William
Butterfield as architect. Part of a reorganisation of Exeter's school system. The Exeter Grammar
School building was erected on land between Barrack and Victoria Park Roads.

131    *Lithograph by and after W. Spreat, 1866, of the North West corner of Cathedral Yard. The Royal Clarence Hotel was built by William Mackworth Praed in 1769 and became the first 'Hotel' in the country by the use of that term in an advertisement taken out in the following year. Alexander Jenkin noted in 1806 that 'in the front is a neat coffee room'. A great rival with the New London Inn as the city's premier hostelry.*

132  *Steel line engraving by J. F. Lambert after W. H. Bartlett, 1830. The Royal Public/Subscription Rooms were built in the 1820s and destroyed in 1942. Many of the city's leading civic occasions took place there. The New London Inn was built in 1794 by John Land. In 1802 Robert Southey noted that there was a sofa and sideboard in his apartment and wrote that these 'articles of luxury;' would no doubt figure in his bill. It was demolished in the 1930s and replaced by a cinema. The buildings were situated in what was called London Inn Square – at the junction of Northernhay Place and North Road near to where the East Gate had stood.*

133  *Pen and ink drawing of the New London Inn, c.1920, not long before it was demolished.*

134   *Photo-tint by James Akerman after a drawing by Silvanus Trevail, 1902. This was an ambitious*
*plan for the Great Western Hotel which was in all likelihood not followed.*

135    *Anonymous lithograph after John Gibson, 1874, of the City Bank with St Petrock's church to the left. The Exeter Bank originally opened in 1769 at the corner of St Martin's Lane and Cathedral Close. It moved to Broadgate a generation later and was extended onto the High Street in the 1870s. The building was by John Gibson, architect.*

136    *Etching by J. Hayward, c.1860. The Devon County Bank was built in Cathedral Close and the building remains a financial institution.*

137    *Anonymous steel line engraved vignette, c.1850. The railway arrived at Exeter on 1 May 1844*
*and within a day small boys were imitating the sound of the steam trains in the streets of Exeter (to*
*the annoyance of those passing by).*

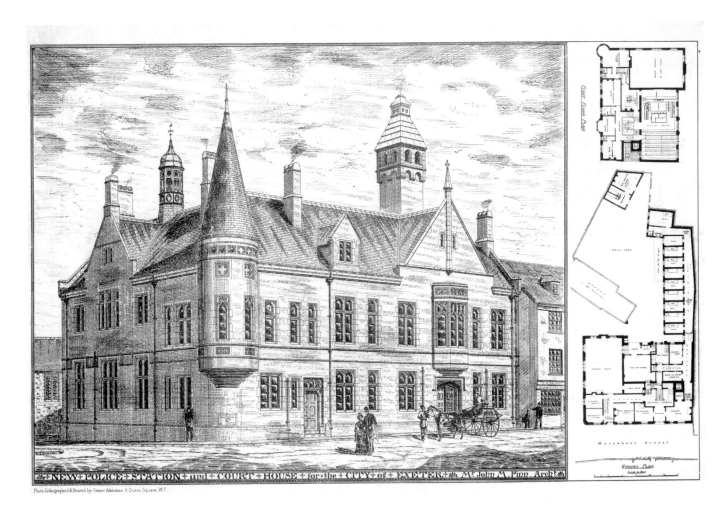

138   Lithograph by James Akerman after a drawing by W.E. Beer, John M. Pinn architect, 1888. The
new police station was built in Waterbeer Street and destroyed in the 1960s.

Business Premises Fore Street and North Street Exeter   BEST AND COMMIN
ARCHITECTS

*139   Lithograph by James Akerman after a drawing by W.E. Beer, 1884. The building, still standing,*
*was erected on the north-west corner of North and Fore Streets. The lettering 'William Brock & Co.'*
*remains on the west side of the building.*

140   *Lithograph by James Akerman after a drawing by Maurice B. Adams, 1883, entitled 'Speranza,*
*High Street, Exeter'. Best and Commin were the architects.*

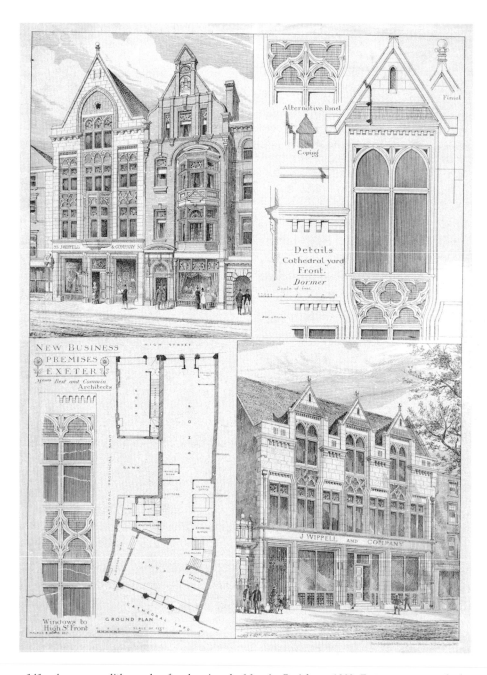

141 *Anonymous lithographs after drawings by Maurice B. Adams, 1883. Entrances were on both High Street and Cathedral Close.*

142    *Possibly a lithograph by W. Hake, 1845. The view is looking west down High Street to the Guildhall. The marchers pass by the Commercial Union Building with its distinctive statue of King Alfred.*

## The Streets and Townhouses

*Eighteen years and more have gone by since the city was devastated. Much has been rebuilt in a commonplace style that might belong anywhere: it is not distinctive as the old Exeter was, with its rich regional flavour. Once more Exeter is the capital of South-Western England, and its shops and streets are as crowded as they ever were. It is still the same kind of city, with seven out of ten of its occupied population providing services of one kind or another. In numbers it grows very slowly, but with the clearing of the congested areas it spreads more and more into the surrounding country. Yet green fields are still visible from most of its streets even today, and it remains one of the most attractive cities in England to look at and to live in. Its two greatest enemies are the motor car and the speculative builder…*

PROFESSOR W.G. HOSKINS, *TWO THOUSAND YEARS IN EXETER*, 1960

143   *Steel line engraving by W. Deeble after T. M. Baynes, 1831. Butchers' Row was built at the turn of the sixteenth century and situated at the top of Smythen Street near to where St George's Market now stands. In 1806 Alexander Jenkins wrote that it 'consists of a narrow street, the buildings, in general, low and mean, with heavy hanging window shutters. Here the knights of the steel reside in a kind of community among themselves, slaughter their cattle and expose their meat for sale… the slaughtering of cattle, with the accumulation of dung, blood &c thrown in heaps behind the houses, makes the Butcher Row a noisome place in the summer'. The row of houses was destroyed over a number of years from just before the first world war to the early 1960s.*

144   *Etching by Frances Margery Hayman, 1927. The entrance of Mary Arches Street is shown leading from Fore Street to St Mary Arches church with its four distinctive stone balls atop the tower.*

145   *Lithograph by H. Besley & Son after G. Townsend, c.1860, of King Street in the West Quarter.*

146 *Etching by Frances Margery Hayman, c.1921, looking down Preston Street
in the West Quarter.*

147    *Anonymous etching of Stepcote Hill, possibly by J. Gendall, 1834.*

148   *Linocut by M.A. Davis, 1928, of the same view.*

Stepcote Hill, possibly originally meaning the Steep Hill, was the main entrance into the city
from the West Gate. It retains its pedestrians' steps on one side and cobbled roadway for
packhorses on the other. The building is represented as being rendered rather than with
exposed timber as it is today.

149    *Etching by NHJ Baird, 1870s, of the bottom of Stepcote Hill showing St Mary Steps Church and the corner opposite before the arrival of the 'House that Moved'.*

150 *Etching by NHJ Baird, 1870s, looking down Stepcote Hill.*

151    *Etching possibly by Neave, 1919, with a bread cart to the right and a shop 'to be let' on the left.*

Before it moved. Number 16 Edmund Street before it moved in 1961 to its current position at the bottom of Stepcote Hill. Built in about 1500, the building is timber-framed on three sides with the remaining wall one of Heavitree stone.

*152    Etching by Nella Delves, 1922.*

153    *Linocut by M.A. Davis, c.1930, providing a third view of the house.*

Numbers 19 and 20 North Street were destroyed at the end of the nineteenth century. The street had a row of merchants' houses with shops on the ground floor.

154    *Engraving after George Townsend, 1873, of Frog Lane below Bridge Street on Exe Island. The House That Moved is possibly depicted to the left.*

155    *Engraving by J.C. Griffiths after G. Townsend, 1873*          156    *Wood engraving by I. Read, 1869*

*157　Etching by NHJ Baird, 1870s*

*158    Engraving by J.C. Griffiths after George Townsend, 1873.*

The statue of St Peter, long one of the features of Exeter, stood at the junction of High Street and North Street, in several locations, for hundreds of years until it was removed and given to Royal Albert Memorial Museum in 1988.

159    *Engraving by J.C. Griffiths, 1873, of the corner of North Street.*

160    *Lithograph by George Palmer, 1867.*

161  *Anonymous wood engraving, 1849, which appeared in* The London Illustrated News. *The election of Lopes to Parliament was prompted by the resignation of Lord Courtenay. The election was held at the Castle and afterwards he processed through the streets preceded by 'The Blue Man', a figure dressed in sky-blue velvet riding upon a white horse also covered in blue cloth. He is depicted here at the corner of High and South Streets. The procession returned to the London Inn for dinner.*

162    *Etching by E.M. Styan, c.1920. Untitled view of houses in Lower North Street.*

163   *Etching by Frances Margery Hayman, 1928. Entitled 'Mermaid Yard, Paris Street'. The Mermaid was situated on Preston Street off South Street.*

164    *Engraving by J.C. Griffiths after George Townsend, 1873, of West Street presumably where the*
*road was overwhelmed by the creation of the Western Way.*

165   *Lithograph by W. C. Featherstone, 1839 of 'Eliot's House'. The early sixteenth-century oriel window of this building in Cathedral Close, probably between St Petrock's church and South Street, was removed and inserted into the Bishop's Palace in the mid-nineteenth century.*

166    *Steel line engraving by J. Greig after J. A. Repton, 1848, of an unidentified house in the city.*

167   *Engraving by J.C. Griffiths after George Townsend, 1873. The Red Lion was situated on Magdalene Street.*

168    *Lithograph by George G. Palmer, 1867, entitled 'Ancient House in Catherine Street, Exeter'.*

*The buildings are no longer standing.*

169    *Etching by NHJ Baird, 1870s*

170   *Etching by Primrose V. Pitman, 1922*

The 'Tudor' House, built in the middle of the seventeenth century, is situated just below the walls on Exe Island. The building is notable for Exeter partly through the elaborate slate-hanging decoration which once extended across a greater portion of the facade.

*171   Engraving by J.C. Griffiths after George Townsend, 1873*

*172   Wood engraving by I. Read, 1869.*

The Chevalier House/Inn, located at number 79 Fore Street, featured a decorative ridge tile of a horseman, still found in some buildings in the South West, notably Marazion in Cornwall. The two buildings were well-known landmarks of the city. They were destroyed in 1942.

173    *Lithograph by Ernest George, 1909.*

174    *Etching by Primrose V. Pitman, 1923.*

*175    Etching by NHJ Baird, 1870s.*

176    *Lithograph by G. Rowe, c.1835. Trehane's sold gin, brandy, wine, etc.*

*177    Anonymous wood cut, no date.*

178   *'Ink Photo' by W.R.L., 1879, of buildings in the High Street.*

179    *Lithograph by Mrs George Rowe, 1835, of houses in the High Street.*

180    *Etching by NHJ Baird, 1870s, also of the High Street.*

182    *Lithograph by W. Spreat,*
*c.1890.*

181    *Lithograph attributed to George Townsend, 1860*

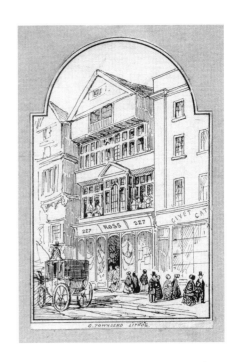

183    *Lithograph by George Townsend,*
*c.1890.*

Three vignettes of buildings in the High Street.

These etchings represent the High Street just before the devastation of the second world war. The views are a reminder of how predominant these early buildings were in the High Street and of how few remain.

*184-6   Etchings by Primrose V. Pitman, 1942*

Mol's Coffee House in Cathedral Close. In 1806 Jenkins wrote that it was 'a very ancient coffee house named Mol's from its first proprietor, an Italian of that name. It is regularly supplied with newspapers and other periodical publications, and is frequented by gentlemen of the first distinction in the city and country'.

187    *Steel line engraving by W. Deeble after A. Glennie, 1830, with St Martin's Church to the left.*

*188   Etching by Primrose V. Pitman, 1925*

The ornately-decorated King John's Tavern stood on the east side of South Street and was demolished in 1834. In 1806 Alexander Jenkins wrote that it was 'vulgarly called King John's Palace'. He also noted that Mr Henry Flashman, the then owner, had greatly altered it and that 'the decorations of the principal entrance are very remarkable, consisting of two grotesque figures, in a crouchant posture, supporting statues; that on the left hand, representing a clown in an antique dress holding a club in the attitude of striking and over his left, on a shield, are the royal arms of England and France, quarterly. The other statue represents a zany, in an antic dress, trimmed with small round bells, his head covered with a long peccadillo cap and holding a child's doll'. In 1881 it was reported that alterations being made to South Street revealed the site and prompted memories of the earlier demolishing of the building when the front was removed and put into storage. The carved figures, depicted here, included men playing a bagpipe and a clarionet as well as two boys wrestling,

189   *Engraving by J.C. Griffiths after George Townsend, 1873.*

Panel of front door
Sketches taken at and after the demolition of the building about 1834.
KING JOHN TAVERN
THE STAIRCASE
E Ashworth
FRONT OF THE KING JOHN TAVERN.
SOUTH STREET EXETER.
E Ashworth

*190 Lithograph by E. Ashworth after a drawing of 1834.*

191   *Etching by T. Mills after F. Wilkinson, 1836. The illustration is of the front door.*

Northernhay can claim to be one of the earliest public parks in the country. Seats were built as early as the first part of the seventeenth century for the citizens who promenaded below the city walls. Northernhay House is shown to the right.

*192    Steel line engraved vignette by Newman & Co, c.1850.*

*193    Steel line engraved vignette after G. Townsend, 1853.*

194    *Lithograph by & after W. Spreat, 1859. The Vineyard, a private house, was situated immediately below the Castle Gate and bought in the early twentieth century. It became a student residence for the University College of the South West of England but requisitioned as a temporary hospital during the first world war. Now known as Bradninch Hall.*

*195   Anonymous steel line engraved vignette, 1865*

*196   Lithograph vignette by G. Townsend, c.1850*

197    Anonymous wood engraving entitled 'Inauguration of the Dinham Statue at Exeter' , 1866. The
statue to John Dinham was made by E.B. Stephens who already had sculpted several statues in the city
including of Sir Thomas Acland. It was reported that the statue 'is said to be a fine work of art but not
a characteristic likeness of the man'. It was paid for by public subscription to honour a man who had
won local esteem through a 'quiet, unassuming disposition, strict integrity as a tradesman and active
spirit of benevolence'. Dinham had bequeathed nearly £24,000 in his will in addition to building a
range of 16 cottages on the land subsequently known as Mount Dinham.

*198    Lithograph by George Townsend, 1840, of the Horticultural Show in Northernhay in 1840.*

199    *Lithograph by & after W. Spreat, c.1845, looking towards St Sidwell's church.*

200    *Lithograph by & after W. Spreat, c.1845, looking out over St David's with the old parish church and Queen Street.*

# The Cholera epidemic of 1832

*Rejoicing in the welfare and advancing prosperity of the city, the writer can say*

*with admiration and gratitude, that vast as its physical improvement has been,*

*its moral revolution has been still greater; and that no reasonable being need*

*seek elsewhere a residence more salubrious, comfortable, polite and friendly.*

THE REVEREND GEORGE OLIVER, *THE HISTORY OF THE CITY OF EXETER*, 1861

The following twenty wood engravings, by R. Hart after Gendall, 1849, were used to illustrate
Thomas Shapter's history of cholera in Exeter. He wrote long captions to accompany each
wood engraving. The outbreak of cholera in the summer of 1832 caused the deaths of more
than 400 people in the city.

201   'The Conduit in South Street'. Shapter wrote that it, together with other buildings behind, so narrowed the South Street, that in 1834 it was taken down, and replaced in 1836 by a handsome granite obelisk, opposite the eastern entrance to the lower market, and from whence issues an abundant supply of water'.

202   'Dipping steps under the Battery'. Shapter wrote 'these steps are situated under the portion of the town wall so termed. The stream is one of the mill leats that flow through the lower part of the city. The whole scene is now much changed, the dipping steps are bricked up on each side, and a perpendicular wall rises from the leat; the houses on the town wall have been removed, by which means a great improvement has been effected, air and light being thus admitted into two of the principal and densely occupied streets of the south-western quarter'.

203  'The Old Shilhay Bridge'. Shapter wrote 'this, being small and inconvenient, was removed in 1833, when the present bridge, which extends over the spot where the cart stands, was erected. The leat here emerges from under the western end of Old Bridge Street; the buildings to the left have now been taken down'.

204  'The Bucket, Hoop, &c of the Water Carrier'. Shapter wrote 'these implements professionally are now no longer in use'.

205  'Rack Close Lane'. Shapter wrote 'this is a very characteristic sketch of what prevailed in 1832. The town walls in the lower part of the city were much built upon and against, for the houses seen upon their summit have one or two stories beneath on the inner side…'

206  'Pump in the Mint'. Shapter wrote 'the archway forms a part of what was once St Nicholas' Priory, and opened into that portion of it, entitled the Hall of St Nicholas and the prior's quarters. Of this Priory there are considerable remains'. He also noted that a resident by the name of Lawler was responsible for uncovering the well: at some time previous to the cholera outbreak an older man had told her that a deep well was covered over on that spot.

207  'The ancient city waterworks'. Situated below Mount Dinham near the Mill on the Exe. Shapter wrote 'Between and above the arches, a stone slab has been inserted, on which are inscribed the names of Jonathan Pyrke, Richard Lowbridge and Ambrose Crowley, the persons who first built the waterworks in the year 1694. In 1835 these waterworks were abandoned, and converted into gristmills. The cliffs at the back is of shillet or that loose kind of slate which surrounds Exeter on its northern side, these cliffs slope down here to the leat, and, higher up, to the river'.

208  'Watering the High Street'. The view is of what is now the Turk's Head with the Guildhall to the right. Shapter wrote 'the houses in the foreground are the remains of old Elizabethan buildings, with their projecting stories, which have been modernised by straight windows; the projecting portion of the Guildhall here seen, and over which is situated the Council chamber…'. He noted the water was 'turned on from the fire plug, ran down the gutters in a full stream, and, being damned up short distances by coils of straw and tarpauling, was collected in considerable quantities. Men with large wooden shovels then threw if plentifully over the neighbouring surfaces. This mode was not only the most effectual as a means of watering the streets, but was most useful in cleansing the gutters. The whole scene, when this was doing, was most striking and picturesque; three or four powerful men, jack-booted, or naked as to their arms and legs, took possession of the street, and stream after stream of water flowed from their well-plied shovels'.

209  'West Gate'. Shapter wrote 'this [wood]cut represents that portion of the town walls between which the ancient West Gate stood; this gate was taken down in 1815. The summits of the walls, as seen in [wood]cut VI [illustration 205] are crowded with small tenements, and the houses built against them are here more particularly shown. In the distance is Stepcote Hill, a steep paved way, and St Mary Steps Church, on the right-hand corner of which is a small vaulted room beneath the church, which was originally occupied as a guard room or lodge for the porter of the West Gate. This is the centre of that district of the city where dwell the greater number of the poorer people, and in which the large amount of mortality from cholera took place'.

210  ' St Mary Arches Street'. Shapter wrote 'here were situated the Soup Kitchen and the Station House, that from which the man is emerging is the latter. This [wood]cut represents one of the streets in the city, in which the buildings of Queen Anne's and more recent times, mingle with those of Edward VI and Elizabeth. The church in the distance is that of St Mary Arches'.

211　'Houses in the Fore Street'. Shapter wrote 'these are interesting and exceedingly good specimens of the old English house; they are still well preserved by the good taste of their owners, and long may they so remain; they were probably built in the early time of Edward VI. On the summit of the further house is a curious figure of a man on horseback, made of a coarse clay pottery. There is a legend that when Prince Charles halted in his adventurous flight into the west (Sept. 1651) after the battle of Worcester, certain diminutive equestrian figures, formed of pottery, were placed on the housetops of every dwelling where he found shelter, in order to denote speed, and give a signal which was well understood by his friends. This can, however, scarcely have been the case here, as he did not upon that occasion proceed further westward than Axminster; still it is not improbable they had some reference to these times, for they were then placed on buildings in each of the large towns; a few years since a house was pulled down at Tavistock, on the roof of which was similar figure. There are other records in Exeter of this prince; his soubriquet of the 'Black Boy', given to him by General Monk, and by which he was known amongst his partisans, gives a name to one of the great outlets of the City'. See Illustrations 171–7.

212　'Goldsmith Street'. Shapter wrote the houses 'on the right were removed in 1834 for the purpose of the Upper Market, which now occupied their site. The house, over the doorway of which is the wagon-headed porch, is of the early time of Elizabeth, if not of that of Edward the Sixth, as in 1568 Mrs Joan Tuckfield bequeathed these premises to the Tailors' Company, who retained it as their hall. The two low gables nearer the church are of rather later date, being Fley's Almshouses, erected in 1638. The penthouses here are worthy of remark. The church is that of St Paul, rebuilt in the reign of William III, and presents the general characters of buildings of this period, being modifications of Roman or Grecian architecture.' The church of St Paul was destroyed in 1936.

213　'Batholomew Yard by Midnight'. Shapter wrote 'the tool house, or vestry as it was sometimes called, has now been removed, together with its centre and lower seat. The inscription which was over the centre has been inserted in a new portion of wall that occupies the site of the tool house'. Shapter also noted that on 16 August 1832 the last burial relating to cholera took place in the graveyard: the burial took place late at night in moonlight and the gravedigger placed the corpse over one of the oldest tombstones in the cemetery near the city wall. According to Shapter the high number of deaths in the city created a need for additional diggers but few men could be found willing to do the work. These men refused to touch the coffin and bribed with extra money and alcohol.

214　'Smythen Street or the Butcher Row'. The illustration shows two tar barrels fumigating the street. Vinegar and lime was also used to cleanse the city. Shapter wrote that the overhangings provided some protection from rain but also threw it into the centre of the street.

215  *'Bridge Street and old St Edmund's Church'. The illustration shows the handcart which was used to transport clothing which had been owned by cholera victims. Initially bedding and wearing apparel were destroyed but later they were cleaned and distributed to the needy. Shapter noted that 'this street is so called from not only communicating with the bridge, but really forming a part of it'.*

216  *'The Shillhay and Quay'. Shapter wrote 'the upright frames seen in the foreground are technically termed 'racks' and are, or I may say were, used in drying and stretching the woollen goods formerly manufactured in the neighbourhood. The operative part of the woollen trade carried on within this city was entirely confined to finishing the pieces for use after they had been spun and wove.*

*From the warehouses within the city the raw materials were distributed into the neighbouring villages, and then returned in the piece. Here the pieces were submitted to a variety of processes, as washing, milling, fulling, dyeing, raising, cutting, hot-pressing, and packing; they were rack-dried after the four first operations. A few years since these racks abounded in the neighbourhood, but are now nearly all gone, as are those here depicted'.*

217  *'The Southernhay burial ground'. The illustration depicts a crowd which gathered at the burial of a man and his wife who lived in James Street. It was popularly believed that the undertaker had acted improperly in his treatment of the deceased husband's body while his widow lay dieing in the same room. Amongst the cries of the crowd at the burial were 'they were buried alive' and 'it was burying like a dog'. Policemen were needed to keep order at the burial. Shapter wrote that the cemetary 'is now closed and planted, and a portion of it was thrown into the public road in 1847. The houses are examples of the poorer tenements which within the last hundred years have been built in the suburbs of the city'.*

218  *'Stepcote Hill'. Shapter wrote that 'at the upper part of the steps to the right is the entrance to one of those courts of miserable houses which then abounded, and which, with others have been now cleared away'. He also gave several case histories of the cholera deaths and this may depict a woman whose child died and 'on the removal of the body the mother fell into great distress of mind, ran through the street as if insane, her hair loose over her shoulders: she continued in a weak state of mind, proclaiming she possessed a charm of a sweet-smelling substance which kept off the disease, until the 17th of August, when she died'.*

219 'Cricklepit Mills'. Shapter wrote 'this represents one of the millstreams that traverse the lower part of the city; to the left is an ancient fulling mill. The houses opposite are of the Elizabethan period; the 'architectural improvements' of the present day have metamorphosed them, they have now square plaster fronts and guillotine windows. On the town wall is seen one of the little tenements whose under stories are built against it'.

220 'Rose and Crown Inn, High Street'. Shapter wrote it 'was taken down in 1834; it was probably built about the time of James I, and is particularly interesting as illustrating the range and character of the houses in the principal street of the city at that period, and which were then for the most part of wood and stone, with high thatched and sometimes slated roofs, they were huddled together in masses, low pitched, small and inconvenient, with here and there a house of greater dimensions. It was then the custom for the merchant to live in the midst of his business, so that the affluent and poor were much mixed together. The two neighbouring houses show the modern character of building which, during the reigns of Georges, has taken the place of them'.

# The Royal Agricultural Society Exhibition, July 1850

*The whole appearance of the city is such as that usually presented in honour of some triumphant destroyer of his species, and this is the first time we have had the pleasure of witnessing a like compliment to the more useful arts of peace.*

THE ILLUSTRATED LONDON NEWS

*The Illustrated London News* printed eight wood engravings of the event and three local newspapers included illustrations of the show grounds, the dining pavilion and of Exeter. There were side shows in addition to the exhibition including a magician at the Theatre Royal, an 'Equestrian Troupe of Ladies', a Grand Concert given by Miss C. Hayes, Cooke's Circus, a Bosjesman's (Bushman's) or Wild Africans' Exhibition and the ascent from the Castle of a balloon from which a cat parachuted to the spectators below.

221　*Wood engraving by F.G. Smyth for* The Illustrated London News. *This 'is a vignette view of the ancient cathedral town. In times of peril it became a 'City of Refuge' and was subjected to many sieges, which it endured with such constancy, always on the side of the Sovereign, that it gained the motto of Semper Fidelis – a mark of character of which the Exonians of the present day are not a little proud'. In the foreground, between the two agricultural labourers and in front of the steam train, are examples of modern farm equipment. These were described as the 'wondrous and strange-looking implements which tear and torture mother earth in these days more than all the convulsions which geologists tell us she suffered in pre-Adamite ages'.*

222 *Wood engraving of Exeter by T. Wragg after R Barrow for* Woolmer's Exeter and Plymouth Gazette.

223 *Exeter from Little John's Cross Hill, St Thomas, by M.U. Sears after Ellis for* The Western Times.

224    Wood engraving by F.G. Smyth entitled 'Arch across Queen Street, Exeter' for The Illustrated
London News. *More than twenty arches were erected and evergreens, streamers, banners and flags
were hung from private and public buildings. This arch in Queen Street was complemented by two
rows of larch trees specifically planted for the occasion.*

*225–8　Four wood engravings by F.G. Smyth for* The Illustrated London News *depicting the arches in the city. Some of the city's arches were decorated with crowns, stars and flags, and others were illuminated at night with gas or variegated lamps. The arches were placed across the main streets as well as some of the minor ones.*

229–35   *A commemorative lithograph by William Spreat was also printed in 1850, in Exeter, to mark the Exhibition. This 'Royal sheet of drawings in double-tinted lithography' was sold for four shillings. It provides views of other arches and its depiction of Fore Street (page 194) gives an indication of the extent to which the city was decorated.*

236–7  *Two wood engravings of the Pavilion for* The Western Times *and (over)* The Exeter Flying Post. *A pavilion was erected at the bottom of Northernhay in Queen Street for a great meal on Thursday, the 18ᵗʰ of July. During the dinner a severe thunderstorm swept over the city and torrents of rain fell but the structure held firm.*

238 *Wood engraving by F.G. Smyth for* The Illustrated London News *entitled 'Arch in the Dinner Pavilion, designed by M. Soyer'. The arch was 17 feet high and 12 feet wide and composed of a large white swan, two turkeys, four geese, four large rabbits, two lambs, two pigs' heads, sic bullocks' heads, four ducks, four hens, one large barn-door cock, six white pigeons, two stags' heads as well as carrots, cucumbers, turnips, cabbages, onions, leeks, corn, fruit, flowers, ribbons and two flags. A plough, rake, hoe and spade were placed on the top. Some 1,200 people attended the meal and consumed 33 dishes of rib beef, 35 dishes of roast lamb, 99 dishes of galantine of veal, 99 dishes of ham, 66 dishes of pressed beef, 2 rounds of beef a la Garrick, 264 dishes of chicken, 33 French raised pies a la Soyer, 198 Spring Mayonnaise Salad, 264 tarts of gooseberries, raspberries and currants, and 198 dishes of potatoes. There were also 33 'Exeter Puddings' which Soyer specially created: it was reported that 'all the matrons of the ancient city were striving to obtain the recipe'.*

239   *Wood engraving entitled 'M. Soyer and the Monster Joint' for* The Western Times. *The food for the occasion was overseen by Alexis Benoit Soyer, the illustrious cook who wrote, three years later in 1853,* History of Food in all Ages. The Western Flying Post *reported that Soyer received a hostile welcome in Exeter because of his politics but that the Frenchman, renamed the 'Gastronomic Regenerator', won over the tradesmen by buying all his supplies locally.* The Illustrated London News *reported that the most novel sight was Soyer's cooking a 'baron of beef' at the Castle. A hole was dug in the Yard and lined with perforated gas pipes from which flames issued forth to cook the meat. The apparatus was designed by Soyer.*

240   *Wood engraving by F.G. Smyth for* The Illustrated London News *entitled 'Roasting the Baron of beef by gas in the Castle-yard, Exeter'.*

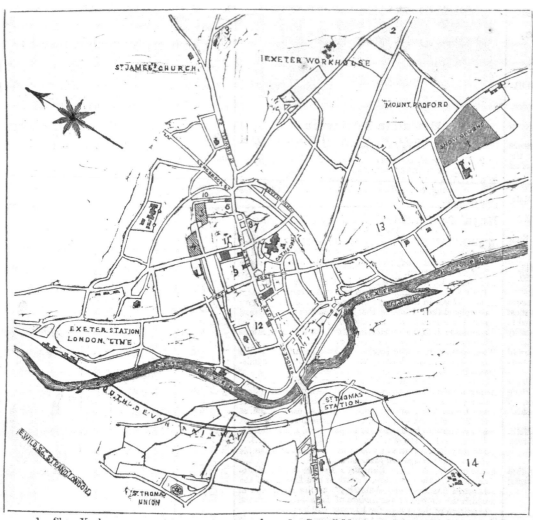

| | |
|---|---|
| 1. Show Yard. | 8. Council Meetings. Sale of Tickets. Secy.'s Room. |
| 2. Roads to Trial Ground, Light Land. | 9. Guildhall. |
| 3. Ditto     Ditto     Heavy Land. | 10. Judges of Assize Room. |
| 4. Dinner Pavilion. | 11. Post Office. |
| 5. Castle Yard. | 12. Western Times Office. |
| 6. Subscription Rooms. | 13. Horticultural Society. |
| 7. Lecture Room, Athenæum, Bedford Circus. | 14. Lucombe Pince and Co.'s Nursery. |

241    *Plan of Exeter by E. Wild for* The Western Times. *The main exhibition showyard was located in Wonford where the Royal Devon & Exeter Hospital is now situated.* The Western Flying Post *reported that it was held in a field 'enclosed on nearly every side by hedgerow elms, the ornament of the Devonshire landscape and the disgrace of its agriculture'.*

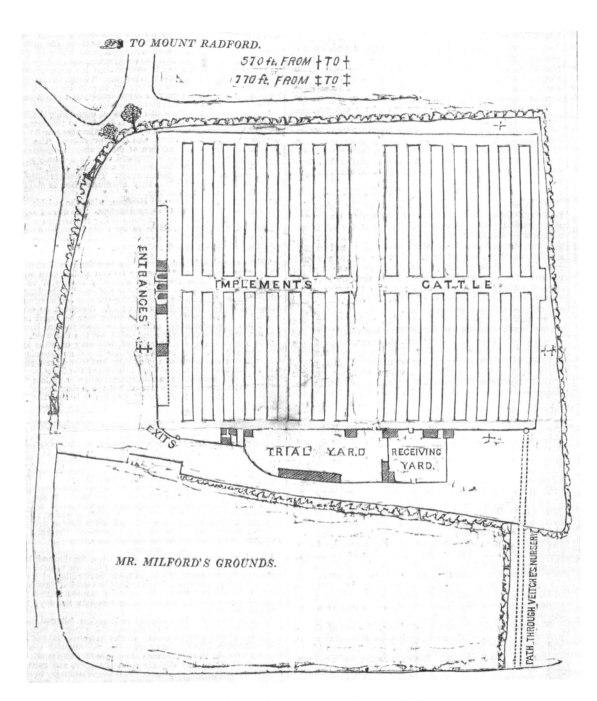

TO MOUNT RADFORD.

570 ft. FROM † TO †
770 ft. FROM ‡ TO ‡

ENTRANCES

IMPLEMENTS

CATTLE

EXITS

TRIAL YARD.

RECEIVING YARD.

MR. MILFORD'S GROUNDS.

PATH THROUGH VEITCH'S NURSERY

242–3   *Plans of showyard for* The Western Times *and (over) for* The Exeter Flying Post.

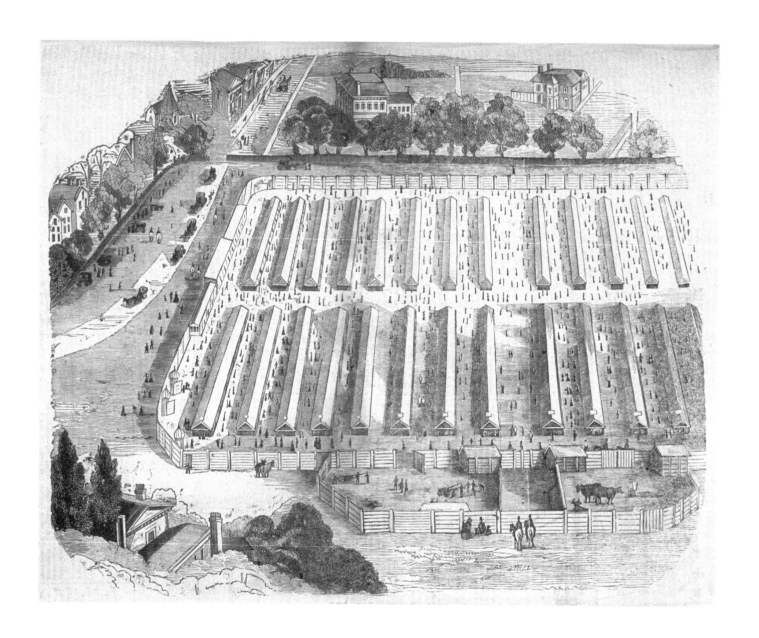

244    *Wood engraving by F.G. Smyth for* The Illustrated London News *entitled 'Arrival of Cattle at the Show-yard'. The paper also noted that 'there was also a considerable influx of the hardy, sun-tanned sons of the soil – men whose talk is ever of the long-horns and short-horns, of Devons and Herefords, of Dartmoors and Leicesters… practical men, who value a tree for the quantity of solid timber it produces, whose 'babble of green fields' relates only to the number of loads of hay to be raised from an acre of land, and whose only care for botany is to ascertain what are the best grasses for fattening their cattle'.*

245    *Wood engraving entitled 'view of the trial grounds' for* The Exeter Flying Post.

*246–7 Two vignettes of Exeter by T. Wragg after T. Haskell of the High Street with the Guildhall and Queen Street with the new Post Office and Higher Market for* Woolmer's Exeter and Plymouth Gazette. *The American Ambassador to Paris was in Exeter for the Exhibition. The Western Flying Post reported him saying that city was 'remarkable for its neatness, the simplicity and good taste of its streets, and dwellings generally, and especially for the kindness and cheerfulness of its inhabitants'.*

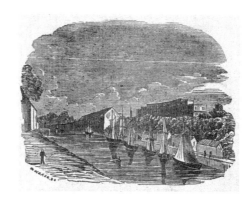

248–50   *Three vignettes of Exeter by T. Wragg after T. Haskell of the Quay and Colleton Crescent;*
*Northernhay and St Sidwell's church; and Bury Meadow, Hele's School and almshouses for*
Woolmer's Exeter and Plymouth Gazette.

# Illustration Sources

Numbers refer to illustrations which, unless otherwise, have a Westcountry Studies Library reference number (WSL) followed by its original source where known.

1-2 WSL, SC925-6: Samuel & Nathaniel Buck, *Antiquities or Venerable Remains of above 400 castles, monasteries, palaces etc in England and Wales*, 1726-52; 3 WSL, SC924: William Stukeley, *Itinerarium Curiosum* (1724); 4 WSL, SC927; 5 WSL, SC928: *The Complete English Traveller* (1771); 6 WSL, SC929: *The Lady's Magazine*; 7 WSL, SC923: Count Magalotti, *The Travels of Cosmo the third, Grand Duke of Tuscany, through England during the reign of King Charles the Second* (1821); 8 WSL, SC931; 9 WSL, SC932: F.C. Lewis, *The Scenery of the River Exe* (1827); 10 WSL, SC934: F.C. Lewis, *The Scenery of the River Exe* (1827); 11 WSL, SC941: TH Williams, *A Guide to the Picturesque scenery and antiquities of Devonshire* (1827-8); 12 WSL, MPr/P&D03784, from a newspaper of 1850 referring, on the back, to the recent death of the Duke of Cambridge of 8 July; 13 WSL, SC942: Thomas Allom, *Devonshire Illustrated* (1829-32); 14 *The Illustrated London News*, 21/8/1869; 15 WSL, SC938: Charles Knight, *The Land We Live In* (1848-50); 16 WSL, SC948: Henry Beasley, *Views in Devonshire* (1848-71); 17 WSL, SC939: J.S & Company, Views (*c*.1855-60); 18 WSL, SC944; 19 WSL, SC946: Newman & Company, *Thirty Views of Exeter and Neighbourhood* (Exeter, *c*.1845); 20 WSL, SC950: J. Harewood, *Scenery of Great Britain* (1841-3); 21 WSL, MPr/P&D40373; 22 WSL, Opr/P&D/ no reference: Newman & Company, *Thirty Views of Exeter and Neighbourhood* (Exeter, *c*.1845); 23 WSL, SC955: CF Williams, *Views in Exeter* (*c*.1835); 24 WSL, SC959: William Spreat, *Views in South Devon* (*c*.1845-50); 25 WSL, SC951: George Rowe, *Views of Exeter* (Exeter, *c*.1828); 26 WSL, SC952: Thomas Allom, *Devonshire Illustrated* (1829-32); 27 WSL, SC953: Thomas Moore, *The History of Devonshire from the earliest period to the present* (1829-30); 28 WSL, SC954; 29 WSL, SC961: Henry Beasley, *Views in Devonshire* (1848-71); 30 WSL, SC960: J. Harewood, *Scenery of Great Britain* (1841-3); 31 WSL, MPr/P&D06583; 32 WSL, SC743: *The Antiquarian and Topographical Cabinet* (1805-1811); 33 WSL, SC765: Kershaw & Son,

*Views* (*c*.1845-60); 34 WSL, SC762: Thomas Allom, *Devonshire Illustrated* (1829-32); 35 WSL, SPr/P&D40277; 36 WSL, SC757: Sherwood & Company, *Devonshire Buildings* (1823-4); 37 WSL, SPr/P&D06868; 38 WSL, SC746: J.M. Turner, *Picturesque Views in England and Wales* (1838); 39 WSL, SC747; 40 WSL, SC748: CF Williams, *Views in Exeter* (*c*.1835); 41 WSL, SC750; 42 WSL, SC752: A Jenkins, *The history and description of the city of Exeter and its environs* (Exeter, 1806); 43 WSL, SC755: C.J.G. Sprake, *Gates and Other Antiquities of the city of Exeter* (Exeter, 1831-2); 44 Royal Albert Memorial Museum, 9/1933.14; 45-7 WSL, SC933, SC744 & SC753: FC Lewis, *The Scenery of the river Exe* (1827); 48 WSL, SC764; 49 *The Illustrated London News*, 14/9/1856; 50 WSL, SC756: John Gendall, *Etched Views of Exeter*, 1834; 51 WSL, SC767, inset on Rocque's map of Exeter, 1744; 52 WSL, MPr/P&D07799; 53 WSL, MPr/P&D03867; 54 WSL, MPr/P&D03886; 55 WSL, SC1005: Henry Beasley, *The Exeter Guide and Itinerary* (Exeter, 1836); 56 *The Illustrated London News*, 19/9/1863, 297-8; 57 WSL, P&D/OPr/ C3884; 58 WSL, SC776; 59 WSL, SC779; 60 WSL, SC768: Francis Grose, *Antiquities of England and Wales* (London, 1773-6); 61 WSL, SC773: A. Jenkins, *The history and description of the city of Exeter and its environs* (Exeter, 1806); 62 WSL, MPr/P&D03873; 63 James Commins, *Antiquities of Exeter*, 1880s; 64 WSL, SC1027: Richard Polwhele, *Traditions and Recollections* (1826); 65 WSL, SC917: Daniel & Samuel Lysons, *Magna Britannia: Devon* (1822); 66 WSL, SPr/ P&D04024; 67 WSL, SPr/P&D03988; 68 WSL, SC907: C.J.G. Sprake, *Gates and Other Antiquities of the city of Exeter* (Exeter, 1831-2); 69 WSL, SPr/P&D07819; 70 WSL, SC918: C.J.G. Sprake, *Gates and Other Antiquities of the city of Exeter* (Exeter, 1831-2); 71 William Cotton, *An Elizabethan Guild of the City of Exeter* (1873); 72-3 WSL, OPr/P&DB4193 & B4191; 74 WSL, SC908: John Britton & Edward Wedlake Brayley, *The Beauties of England and Wales* (1809), IV; 75 WSL, SC910: Daniel & Samuel Lysons, *Magna Britannia: Devon* (1822); 76 WSL, SC911; 77 WSL, SC912: C.J.G. Sprake, *Gates and Other Antiquities of the city of Exeter* (Exeter, 1831-2); 78 Cotton, *An Elizabethan Guild*, 1873, 50; 79-80 WSL, SC913-14: John Gendall, *Etched Views of Exeter*, 1834; 81 WSL, SC898: Daniel & Samuel Lysons, *Magna Britannia: Devon* (1822); 82 WSL, SC896: *The*

VICTORIA PARK

VIEW ON THE EXE.

COUNTY GAOL

NEW NORTH ROAD

ST DAVIDS CHURCH

CASTLE

NORTHERNHAY

CATHEDRAL

BISHOPS PALACE

MACDALENE STR

GREAT SHILHAY

PAINTERS ROW

POST OFFICE